Vengeful Hymns

Poems by

Marc J. Sheehan

The Ashland Poetry Press
Ashland University
Ashland, Ohio 44805

Printed in the United States of America

ISBN: 978-0-912592-67-1

LCCN#: 2009903689

Book cover design by Mike Ruhe

Cover art by Marc J. Sheehan

Author photo by Bill Bitzinger

Thank you to the editors of the following journals in which these poems, some in earlier versions, first appeared:

Atlanta Review, "The Clumpiness Factor"
The Burning World, "On the Passing of the Great Picture Palaces"
Controlled Burn, "Rhubarb"
Driftwood, "On Being Rumpled" and "Genealogy"
Fine Madness, "Deconstruction"
Full Circle, "Census 2000"
FutureCycle Poetry, "Detour outside Walhalla, Michigan" and
    "The Fishermen"
I Stay Home, "Losing the Farm"
Jabberwock Review, "Rental History"
Louisville Review, "The Apollo Missions"
The MacGuffin, "Blue Ribbon"
Mediphors, "Actuarial"
Nebraska Review, "Job Accomplishments"
Passages North, "The *Sun,* The *Star, et al.*"
Prairie Schooner, "Vernal Equinox near the 45th Parallel"
Prairie Star, "The Evolution of the Martini" and "Song"
Slant, "Signing the Blues"
Southern Poetry Review, "A Note on Rejection," "The Ontology of
    Morning in Moveen, County Clare," "Basho in Autumn,"
    "Per Se," and "The Musical Fountain"
Steam Ticket, "Some Notes Concerning Love and *Hemmings Motor
    News*"
the strange fruit, "A Postelection Walk along the Lake"
Switched-On Gutenberg, "The Kitchen"
Water~Stone, "Journeyman" and "With Love from Galveston, Texas"
West Branch, "Driving through Nebraska"
White Pelican Review, "The Dancing Girls of Blind River"

"A Note on Rejection" also appeared in *Don't Leave Hungry: Fifty Years of Southern Poetry Review.*

for Sue William Silverman

Contents

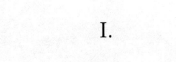

I.

The Back Roads

What you need is a midlife crisis-mobile
with precision rack-and-pinion steering
for cornering these ninety-degree turns

past farmhouses that were in ruin thirty
years ago, ruined still and still lived in
even though their porch roofs have collapsed.

Junked cars with halos of unmowed grass
guard modular homes prewired with failure,
and the abandoned Pentecostal church

could be bought for a hymn. Yard sales display
chipped bric-a-brac on folding tables,
tarnished swag left out for weeks and covered

by tarps like outsized magicians' handkerchiefs.
Yank them away and you'd expect to see
entire flocks of carefully stuffed white doves.

You could buy yourself everything you need
to be someone else—unreflective mirrors,
bladeless razors, an hourglass made from

empty fifths of whiskey glued together
mouth to mouth as if kissing, except not.
You're you, though, and the road straightens out,

so you speed past the battered stands of fresh
vegetables, the orchard of blueberries
whose fruit you're offered only if U-Pick.

Like happiness, you think, as it shrinks away.

Detour outside Walhalla, Michigan

I was thinking about other things back then
so I didn't see, there past the Road Closed sign
I'd driven around, how a washed-out bridge makes
the space over a river emptier
than where there was never a bridge at all.
But don't blame me for that—I had yet to lose
a job, a wife, certain weekends, the wicker
creel I used to keep drafts of poems in.
After all, I didn't cause the flood.
Is it my fault all those letters stored in
the basement bloom with mold like the mottled
bodies of salmon floating back downstream?
Look—see that late-season Coho pushing
itself over the sandbar? From such high banks
lumbermen rolled logs into the river
until you could have walked straight across like Christ,
had Christ not given a damn about anything.
As for me, I just stood at the edge a while,
the engine idling and night taking root
in second-growth oak and rows of pine trees
planted to make work during the thirties.
When I was finally good and ready,
I turned around and went where I was told
to go—although not all the way to hell,
just the next rickety bridge downriver
on the Pere Marquette. Wait, that's not true.
It was daylight, the next bridge was sturdy,
and the calm north fork flowed well within its banks.
As for my goodness and readiness, let
me just say that I'm watching my step,
Sweet Jesus, and praying only for the sun
to burn my lost self here a while longer.

4

Vernal Equinox near the 45th Parallel
3/20/03

The weather has turned warm suddenly, melting
the snow banks, driving sap in maples, herding deer
along their annual, mysterious paths.
Because of this, body after body,
freshly hit or newly thawed from drifts,
line the highway—delicate necks stretched back,
alarmingly white bones jutting at odd
angles from out of hides turning gray.
Maybe it only *seems* worse than usual,
but then how to account for Crow's ecstasy?
I tell him we're here, in this moment balanced
between dark and light, equator and pole.

He just flaps his black wings and keeps feeding.

The Dharma Body

We were tired of learning things from books.
We'd read *Electric Kool-Aid Acid Test*,
read *Doors of Perception, The Teachings of Don Juan*,
so we scored some peyote
and when my parents went on vacation
we drove to their place—the countryside seeming
like a better place to trip
than our warren of student rentals.
Beautiful, fearless Amy sat at a weathered picnic table,
opened the plastic bag of buttons,
then popped one in her mouth.
I was in bad shape that summer, having broken
up with a girlfriend, passed out
under hypnosis, and perfected the pleasure of drinking bourbon
straight up, which is where I was suddenly headed
after eating the smallest button in the bag.
I felt as if I were rising in an elevator of air.
Then I lost my breakfast in the bathroom
and took a slug of rum to chase away the taste.
Outside, everything became different in its sameness.
Did I want to know the secret or not? the sun
asked me through my illusory skin.
I walked down the gravel road to get away
from myself, and found myself wandering
through a field of corn stubble, following
a row for a ways before angling off
toward a distant church steeple or abandoned barn,
trying to find my path. Back at the ranch house,
Amy and Jeff and Mikel were across the street
sitting in the tall grass (Dylan's image
for heaven that year), forming an odd little
gallery for the golfers, who didn't seem to mind.
I discovered I wasn't Huxley, Ram Dass, or Casteneda.
So only a few questions remain, like why there wasn't
a new crop of corn in the ground,
where the hell my friends have gone,
and why I didn't follow.

The Crown Chakra

All that winter I stood on the back porch steps
smoking poorly hand-rolled cigarettes
and feeling heat from my bald head—that yogic
center of spiritual strength—rise into
another gray Michigan winter.
My wife had left me and Lansing behind,
her own Crown Chakra opened up to God,
her mystic third eye wide and unblinking
in Arizona's pure and cleansing sunlight.
I felt the bright January stars pour down
their coldest ideas right through my thick skull
as mercury plummeted past zero
in the ancient rusted thermometer.
In response, I donned a blaze-orange toque,
which smelled of mothballs from the cedar chest
the ex left behind, and tried to make my Heart
Chakra open since it was already broken.
But despite being pummeled, it remained
a selfish piñata, keeping its treasures
to itself, the way Humphrey Bogart did in
The Treasure of the Sierra Madre.
I, myself, felt done in, hunted by
misfortune, as if the moths of sorrow
were eating away at my threadbare soul.
And then, despite my best efforts, it was spring.
So I swept up the butts, tossed out my pouch
of Drum tobacco, tapered off my crying
jags to once a fortnight, and looked hard into
the mirror, hoping to find the bright aura
of healing and well-being haloing me.
Still, I put away my cap and darkest thoughts
and went bareheaded out into April,
flesh balancing spirit, a commoner
in the secret kingdom of the resolute.

Driving through Nebraska

Outside Ogallala, there's a rise with a sign
warning you to watch for wind
on the bridge, as if you were Vincent,

who saw it in huge blue swirls
curling around the stars above Arles.
Except that here the sky seems too small

to cover the miles and miles of Nebraska
flat as the earth before Copernicus.
Or maybe Nebraskans can see angels.

Maybe the gazers into crystal balls
all call Omaha their home.
These are the kinds of thoughts that haunt you

when you stop the truck to piss and consider
how full of Nebraska Nebraska is,
how there are people who live without regret

even in Nebraska! They say,
"I just can't see being blue," and
"That's just water under the bridge."

To think on these things helps to bring
the soul into a state of grace—
and the body with another hour's drive to Wyoming.

The Clumpiness Factor

While waiting in the Las Vegas airport for
    the redeye flight to Cheyenne, laying over
        to save money on her trip west,
Diane had the Clumpiness Theory explained
    to her by a Radio Shack clerk.
        Once one customer finally decides
to buy a battery or patch cord,
    then everyone else suddenly makes up their mind
        to buy that laptop, modem, or phone.
Then there's a void filled by straightening shelves
    before the next customer comes in.
        This, in miniature, is the principle behind
quarks forming atoms, atoms molecules,
    molecules matter, matter planets,
        planets solar systems, solar systems galaxies,
and galaxies super-galaxies.
    It's also why I gave Diane
        a dollar to play the Vegas airport's slots
in hopes a whole clump of money would come tumbling out.
    No such luck, I'm sorry to say.
        So, to what have I been a more magnetic center?
Thistle burrs and their sister seeds.
    Rained-on clay that after cloudbursts make
        my lightweight running shoes almost unliftable.
A fine supply of not-yet-dried-out pens stashed in
    a hunter's discarded cartridge box.
        Papers, letters, fragments, and drafts.
Dreams that leave their disquieting outlines
    like the mud-rings of sun-dried puddles.
        Stones that always manage to lose their luster
once I pluck them from water.
    And words, never quite the right ones—
        clay the creator trimmed from the swift.

Postcard from Hadley to Miss Katherine Newman, Hart, Michigan, Cancelled Jan. 30, 3:00 p.m., 1911, in Kalamazoo, Mich.

Leave Kazoo this
week, to roam
got my desire
going to be a
Traveling Man.
Hurrah—Now
I will get
all that is
coming to me.
Good bye.

Rental History

Who planted the Japanese
ornamental, who the blue
spruce, lilacs, the two
      unpruned ragged apple trees?

Some faded plastic markers
proclaim eggplant and tomato.
What tenant years ago
      left behind this garden

whose perennials now are
goldenrod, thistle, and burdock?
Stacked behind unfastened locks
      are empty Mason jars.

The yard's mostly weeds;
apples ripen into pears.
Moldy beneath basement stairs
      are catalogs of seeds.

On Being Rumpled

I didn't know until I went to wash
my clothes at the laundromat that what I want
is to build a backyard screen house with plans
from a discarded *Family Handyman*.
Didn't know how much I long to level
6x6 treated beams over a trough
of gravel, and fasten notched upright
posts to the outer foundation. Hadn't
guessed my wish to install joists at each end,
aligning the ends of other joists with string.
How could I have known that I want to nail
5/4 x 5½ inch decking
to the tops of the joists with 10d nails?
Who knew I'd want to screw the inner headers
flush with the top of the posts? And the very
thought of nailing rafters to the ridge all
but makes me miss my turn for a dryer.
So imagine the joy in cutting compound
angles for the hip and the jack rafters,
then nailing them together with 8d nails,
which then I'd cover with cedar roof boards,
plywood, and number 2 cedar shingles.
How fine to rout laps for the door frame joists,
assembling each door squarely, then cutting
and stapling aluminum screening in
and finishing with decorative molding.
I ache to install the floor cleats even
with the outer edges of the posts so
I can have each door, trimmed at top and bottom,
fit snugly from the floor to the header.
Already I can feel the free-swinging doors
kept in place by their self-closing hinges.
And what satisfaction I'd have attaching
the curved cedar brackets with galvanized screws.
I lack only my own place, talent, power
tools, patience, and thirty-five hundred

dollars worth of lumber. And so I'll head
back with my hamper of unfolded clothes,
still dreaming of gazebos and jig saws,
still puzzling out just how I might
otherwise make my rented heaven whole.

Deconstruction

I'm lifting weights in the basement—bench presses—
when I notice the way the first floor's
underside is braced: diagonal boards above the beams, and the beams
themselves braced by mitered 2x4s crossed
like the bones beneath Jolly Roger's skull,
the whole of it clean and Euclidean,
intricate as a train trestle, those old ones
which in photographs of the first trans-Canada look
very like a patient child's work with glue and match sticks.

At this point in a poem, the poet is reminded
of other kinds of braces: those on teeth
perhaps, then those for legs crippled
by birth, accident, or acts of God. This is how you segue
from orthodontics to ontology.
Think of the story about Martin Guitars
and their secret warehouse for instruments braced
inside in strange ways which resonate so deeply
even the thick- and splay-fingered could move us.

Then one says something about the body's bracing and how
we are not built for such wear as the world requires of us,
we with our same old biblical ribs and spines of crooked dice.
But parts of us, hidden beneath the flesh, are
so intricate (think of an anatomy class's skeletal hands and feet)
that one feels, putting hand to fretboard or foot to creaking floor,
that creation was at play when making something work
with this many moving parts, for such a short time,
it's true, but fluid nonetheless,

above its bones, below its tattoos and bruises.

The Kitchen

1.
How many times have you ended up past midnight in the light of the refrigerator? If Edward Hopper's nighthawks had kitchens, they wouldn't be so famously blue.

2.
Even though there's caviar, lox, and baguettes on the dining room table, the guests still gather in the kitchen amid empty bottles and the turkey's picked-over bones.

3.
A meal has already been prepared for the priest brought in to bless the house.

4.
Recipes for which you lack saffron or oyster sauce are seductive as travel brochures and their unreal photographs of happiness.

5.
We leave the womb twice—once from our mother's body, and once from her kitchen.

6.
How strange the kitchen is after the funeral. No one can find the gravy boat, the pickle fork, the candles salvaged from the last birthday cake.

7.
Who would think to list in an obituary that the kitchen outlives its cook?

Colander

The utensil in its Platonic, almost abstract form is, like other tools, an intermediary between humans and the world. Heidegger said that, I think, although he didn't use a colander as an example. Certainly not this particular colander bought years ago at a garage sale. The holes punched in it form six-cornered stars like Stars of David or the pattern for Chinese checkers. Real stars, we now know, are more amazing and less lovely—or is it more beautiful and less mythic? To be useful, this planetarium has to be turned upside-down. Potatoes are the earth apples cleansed of dirt in its cradle. That colander got lost in some move or went to Tucson with the ex-wife; the new one is blue plastic, strictly business. It has none of the past's loveliness that comes after memory has washed over events, leaving only what it cares to remember.

The Recipe Box

At first, everything is ordered by course—appetizers, side dishes, salads, entrees, desserts—and written carefully on 3x5 cards, of which there is a generous helping of extras. Then clippings from food magazines slip in, along with family secrets scribbled unintelligibly for one or the other of you on carefully folded sheets of onionskin. The favorites become spattered with pancake batter, red wine, habanero sauce, or marked with sticky fingerprints. Soon, it's packed tight as a cartoon suitcase, so that the plastic latch can't snap shut. You should try to cull the excess, but are afraid you won't know where to stop. Easier to quit cooking as much and eat out more, now that you can afford it—which is what you wanted all along, isn't it? Then explain your craving for the *pad thai* she used to make for you, or the crepes you made for her, even your former mother-in-law's heavy potato dumplings. Each menu produced a miraculous amount of leftovers, which you can't help but keep eating.

All the Amenities
for Bill Reader and Keith Taylor

Once, needing a place to rent, I called a phone number in a classified ad for a house that seemed promising, or at least affordable. The owner described the one-bedroom by saying that it didn't have many anemones, by which I knew she meant that it was a pretty Spartan place and not that its flower beds weren't doing well. Although maybe they weren't, who knows, since I never went to see. Reading translations of the Greek poet Karyotakis brought back that memory: *Violets and anemones, forgotten / in foreign flower beds, where you perish.* He was in despair at having to work an office job, one that kept getting him transferred farther and farther away from Athens, which contributed to his suicide. Before fatally shooting himself, Karyotakis tried drowning, but kept coming up for air despite his best efforts. Which makes it seem more reasonable, somehow, that it was always sea anemones I imagined that Midwestern rental house lacking. Still young, I wasn't looking for hot tubs or sub-zero freezers. All I wanted was a study from which to send out into the world poems whose self-addressed envelopes would return stuffed with fame. That's the kind of anemone I wanted—something bright and otherworldly—attainable, perhaps, if I had just held my breath long enough, like a child throwing a tantrum. But now, instead, I help a workman pull the butcher-block countertops out of the kitchen to get ready for new ones. Sure, it's a provincial luxury, but I can afford it, and I'm still here to enjoy it. Provincial miracles, but what the hell? Winter is late coming this year, and in the garden the former owner kept up so much better than I do, the cherry tomatoes planted too late could still ripen. How fine they'd look, more lovely than flowers, against the black granite!

II.

Census 2000

Paid by the hour, plus mileage, to find
who hasn't sent in his form, as well as count
the prisons, the migrant camps, handicap
group care, convents, rectories, and nursing homes,
I'm otherwise unemployed and don't care
to think about growing old myself, sharing
a room with an aging, almost-rock-star
flabby in his spandex, cocking his head
to hear something beyond his ringing ears.
I have my badge, a plastic briefcase and

a fistful of stubby pencils for filling
in the little boxes empty as years.
A decade from now my body, please God, will
still be home to my soul, allotting me
a spot on government rolls, a congressman
I didn't vote for, highway funds, public
bathrooms and art, a jury of working peers—
all the civic mysteries, plus a return
address with a seasonal view of the lake,
or the future, or else the sound of waves.

Job Accomplishments

"Born to make minimum wage."
—Bart Simpson

Unlike my cousin, I didn't slash open
my leg with a machete-like knife while
pruning pine trees into holiday shape.
In none of my Freshman Composition
classes did I ever make any student
so sick of the English language that they
never wrote another word ever again.
At least, I never received any letters
to that effect. Affect? I've forgotten.
When I counseled people about just what
their blood tests meant, more often than not
they thanked me for telling them they were sick.
I'm not making this up. And I managed
the books for a company during a time
when I didn't balance my own checkbook,
although the accountant just shook his head.
I painted buildings without falling off
ladders or peeping into apartments,
and worked at an art museum, but not long
enough to find out what painting I was
supposed to save in case of a fire.
So what if it doesn't equal a career?
So what if I never made enough money
to play much golf on the course I helped build
by harvesting stones and sowing bent grass?
At least the hypnotist I assisted gave
me my pick of silver Zippo lighters
smokers had turned in at his suggestion
without even using a pendulum watch.
The trick is to never look down, or back.
Because time's wingèd chariot, or something,
might be gaining, and you can still fall even
when you think you're on solid ground. Trust me,
I know; I haven't done all this for nothing.

Journeyman

Hiding Spenser's *The Faerie Queene* under
the cover of *Soldier of Fortune* or
Swank, I was distracted from those stanzas
by pink or flayed flesh, or the union steward
who rousted us out of our kerosene-
heated shack into a cold October
rain to pace the sidewalk with our signs.
We weren't striking for higher wages,
but for certain language in the contract.
It was my first job after getting married,
and since I could sleep in late and get strike pay,
I was hoping for that strange hiatus
to go on until I found a better job,
or won the lottery, or learned—like an
industrial-strength William Blake—to see
the universe in a grain of casting sand.
What I couldn't see was my own life clearly.
After all, I was young enough to think
we were just what we seemed, because or
in spite of having to learn how to read
blueprints, micrometers, signs that the foreman
had been out at the White Rabbit late last night.
Twenty years later, I still own a few tools
I bought for that job, a union withdrawal card,
divorce papers, and my copy of Spenser
that doesn't even have a bookmark to show
where I gave up trying to make sense of it all.

With Love from Galveston, Texas

When you stand on the granite jetty, looking
out over the Gulf of Mexico at oil
tankers lined up along the horizon
waiting to enter the channel to Houston,
the thought of leading a criminal life
buoys up, unbidden—the desire to steal
someone else's identity to run
up a small fortune in credit card debt,
or dabble in smuggled antiquities,
or learn the myriad ways carnival
barkers have for shortchanging the rubes.
After all, where has being good gotten you,
but here—staring out at the Gulf, wondering
what name you'd take as an alias?
Why not jump in and swim to The Balinese
whose lookouts once kept watch for Rangers
coming to raid the illegal casino
shining brighter than stars out on its pilings.
Now, its gift shop displays blown-up, grainy
photos of famous entertainers who sang, told
blue jokes, or impersonated each other.
There's a plastic roulette wheel and a dead
spotlight that once had Sinatra in its sight,
while outside sunlight breaking through the clouds
illuminates the opaque gray water.
Turning back toward land, you know the only
person you will ever be is yourself—
in case you hadn't figured that out yet.
Later, strolling along the historic Strand,
you'll stop outside an army surplus store
and duck in to buy some black leather gloves,
which fit perfectly as another life.
Wish you were here, and for the moment you are.

Redemption at Lake Forest Cemetery

An inmate crew on lunch break mills
around a cinder-block garage—
the institutional orange

of their undershirts visible
below the short sleeves and open
necks of rough brown work shirts proclaims

prisoner more viscerally
than "Ottawa County Jail" inked
across their broad and shapeless backs.

Above us, a crow casts swift and
graceful shadows on the stones while
Lake Michigan glitters beyond

a dune dotted with cottages.
Banished from the waves, one convict
stretches out on a sun-warmed slab

of cement contentedly as
a snake or a granite lamb and longs
to sprout a pair of unclean wings.

A song about love gone bad wafts
from a dump truck's cab. The tableau
they form is perfect, even though

they are not. They don't care. They have
court-ordered acts of contrition
to perform—galling, thankless tasks.

Per Se

While not a mover *per se*, I once lugged
a full-sized couch single-handedly up
a flight of stairs. I, therefore, have some hope

the will that I wrote can hold up in court,
although I suspect I'll be past caring
based on the mail-order ordination

a friend bought me as a Christmas gift.
Item: For months, I cut what hair I have
using a hand-mirror and blunt scissors.

Hardly anyone laughed. And on the shoulder
of the road, I popped my car's hood to brood
with grave concentration over the engine.

Then when I woke up temporarily
unsure of who's president and whether
it mattered, the CAT scan of the apple-halves

of my brain came back looking fine to me,
able to see clearly the latent desire
but not one seed of rot; yet someone

insisted on a second opinion.
It was almost yogic, the way I held
my breath as I pondered some leftover part,

praying for everything I'd fixed for good.

The Improvisations

Once I win the lottery, I plan
to buy a car with a side-view mirror

that doesn't need a golf tee to keep it in place.
Still, most players on the tour will tell you

recovery is the money shot, the one
they never had to hit until that minute.

True, no one intentionally drives
the ball in the rough, but, nonetheless,

a bent wire clothes hanger better dangles
a pail of paint from a ladder rung than

gizmos designed for just that task,
and a Boy Scout knapsack serving as a sling

got me hauled up to the top of the mast
just fine—twice, in fact, since I mis-rigged

the sail's fouled line the first time I tried.
A wrong first note can doom you, Jarrett said;

you can't always count on that second chance.
So I trimmed carefully a poster for

a show of Kandinsky's *Improvisations*
to make it fit a frame. Gone now, I think

of that abstract sea battle while watering
the garden holding my thumb over the hose-end

after yet another spray nozzle breaks.
The roses don't mind, nor the wildflowers—

entirely different ones this year.

For John Fahey
1939–2001

You died in the year the future was supposed
to arrive. I remember that in part

because a tape of yours played in my clunker's
cassette deck while I stopped to relieve myself

behind some rural church on the way to beg
for my next temp job. I wish I could tell

you how I felt with the dew on my shoes
and the car door open like a broken wing

and your guitar pouring out in full throat.
God knows why they hired me. Every day

your music comes to me from farther away,
the eye of your Martin winks more darkly.

Once, like Bukowski, I believed that money
is piss, and I spent an entire unemployed

summer trying to learn one of your songs.
The calluses that were my payment for that

I pissed away on a comfortable life.
Not you. Grizzled, American, primitive,

and consigned now to the past, you live on
in your music, haunting and accusing.

Blue Ribbon

Head, Heart, Hands, and *Health* are the four H's.
This snapshot's a part of my sister's project—
a gelding that's her whim and which in six
years will be wildly unrideable, God knows,
though now he's so docile that father drops
the halter to have both hands ready to pluck
me, his sunburned peck of pink fruit, from
this long-legged, muscle-shivered cradle.
I hold on to the leather horn as though
I'm ready to break this wild bronc, this life.
The horse holds its breath, a trick for keeping
the saddle from being cinched good and tight.
Its curried tail flares softly in the wind;
the barn doors are opened to chaff-flecked light.
A rope to hang a worn tractor tire swing
comes down plumb from a blue, cloudless sky.
From *Heaven,* the parish priest believes. I think
I will hold on for as long as I can.

Losing the Farm

Forty years and more away from it now,
the animals grow smaller and smaller,

until even the stallion's great droppings
are tinier than those of fleas I comb

out of the coat of my adopted tom.
And now that it can't be divided any finer,

mothers cup hands against windows, hoping
to see their feral children lope home.

Where I'm From

I'm sitting in a lounge on Central Park South
ordering absinthe now that it's legal again,
at least in certain parts of the country,
although perhaps without wormwood enough
to compel drinkers to cut off ears or
stare into the inner light of sunflowers.
And I want to tell the barmaid wearing
a low-cut black dress who serves it to me
without a smile that where I'm from you have
to be nice, because even people who don't
wear Armani, even people who buy
bait shops and fall in love with taxidermists
might be who you call when your life falls apart.
Want to tell her that my mother's named Elvis
and that before my father died he bought
a whole side of beef as a sign of his love—
frozen and packaged neatly as sadness
it crushed the springs of my compact hatchback
and lasted for months after he was gone.
Want to tell her that when the preacher laid hands
on my ex-wife she fell down laughing in tongues,
and that work-release felons once helped me
move in to a furniture museum
where I lived until an attic full of bats
drove me and my cat, Mr. Boston, out.
But she looks as if she's heard it all before.
Someone with such practiced weariness should know
that the right way to serve absinthe is with
a carafe of water, sugar cubes, slotted
silver spoon, and a sense of history.
The glass of sugar water she gives me
in lieu of romance and ritual doesn't
seem to make the absinthe louche quite right,
but I don't complain. You don't where I'm from—
a place with its own attractions but lacking
green fairies, and sirens who reseal

bottles labeled *Lucid* from which you can
only afford to have her pour you one,
even though clearly you could drink it all night.

Genealogy

On the cliffs outside of Kilkee, County Clare,
fresh rivulets falling to the sea
are lifted by the wind and driven inland,
back over the narrow road running between
private fields and a strip of common land.
Sometimes, a grazing cow wanders too close
and falls a hundred meters down to the shore.
Sometimes, sunshine builds rainbows all along
the coast road. Any woman who you meet
might have a Holstein skull in her bathtub,
and secret places to hunt for crystals.
And if the pub keeper owns that grassy field
a primitive, Druidic shrine to Virgin
Mary is built on, who else would you think
collects the coins from the offering jar?
Better to get some Guinness in return.
Better to find your own stones. Better yet,
whiskey on the side, mixed with red lemonade
for sweetness, and to pretend that you belong.

The Ontology of Morning in Moveen, County Clare
for Tom Lynch

The crow has opinions about things and is
not afraid to proclaim them. So does
the little black-and-white songbird whose name
you'd know if only you were more awake.
Unseen, the ocean's blue voice is muffled
by a mile of fields green between stone fences.
Its musical sound rises and falls,
urgent and almost intelligible
as voices overheard behind closed doors.
Or maybe it's talking plainly in Gaelic.
The truth is that you really can't say just what
the waves are saying, or what the nameless
black-and-white songbird sings from the top of
the peat shed's peaked gray roof, or what the crow
crows about with such certainty all morning.

Rhubarb

Among the food the mourners brought,
a rhubarb pie. I'd forgotten its sweetly
bitter taste, how I used to cut the stalks
with a knife sharpened almost away.

This was in the Midwest,
where I was surprised to find a woman
who knew what every line of my hands meant,
even down to the wrinkles around my wrists.

But her predictions didn't come true, praise God.
And now along with haggis, and tea
brewed from the water of Loch Ness,
we cook a black kettle of stewed rhubarb.

The French girl whose ridiculous shoes
made her stumble across the heather
chops up the blood-colored stalks
then cups her hands around a mug of steam.

The wrinkle-bracelets around my wrists predict
I will get to where I've already arrived,
this shore on which Welsh travelers bless
our sour dessert in their lovely tongue.

Signing the Blues

Right in front of the outdoor stage are
the differently-abled, who used to be

the lame, the deaf, the crippled, and the blind.
They have canes, crutches, and motorized wheelchairs.

At the eastern edge of the field, a full moon
is asking for attention or forgiveness.

A young woman translates a song's lyrics,
forming graceful shapes of sadness with her hands.

During the solos, she sways a little bit,
waiting for the singer to start in again.

She overly-mouths the words of the song.
But the words are so big anyway—*cry*

love gun night whiskey guilty baby why—
she's only, really, doing them justice.

Our applause is a thunderous rustle
of leaves. Then a young man stands in her place,

his hands together, almost prayerful, ready
to carve the next vengeful hymn into the air.

Field Guide to the Native Emotions of Michigan
for David James

No, the creator did not shape the state
setting his hand down in blessing, but from
trying hard to save himself from the fall.
And the upper peninsula? A useless
appendage, a cartoon superhero's
power ray unable even to stun
Wisconsin. I can say this since I live here—
have my whole life, if you can believe that.
Man Lives Entire Life in Michigan,
a tabloid headline too terrible to buy.
Imagine shoveling your car out after
an overnight snowstorm—there you are, sweating,
icicles forming on your moustache, the sun
suddenly so bright that even if you knew
where you were going you'd be too blind to drive.
Who was it who said that you should commit
a work of art as though committing a crime—
even a stupid one, like breaking into
a hunter's cabin and getting away
with nothing more than a sack of canned fruit
and half-empty box of .22 shells?
Afterwards, it would help to have at least
a can opener, gun, or alibi.
Why go on living there? you ask. But then,
why *not* go on living here? A question
a long-ago glacier might have scoured
down to its essential: Why not go on
living? Why not go on? Why not go? Why
not? Why? My answer consists of which
finger I'm holding up inside this mitten
and my superhuman resistance to
the rays of loneliness, silent as radon,
whose torments I so bravely withstand. Ask all
my closest friends. He'll tell you the same story.

III.

A Note on Rejection

When I first fell in love with my ex-wife,
I'd take the Amtrak train to Chicago
and must have passed the same backyards that Tunis
Ponsen spent his whole life painting, though it's hard
to stay in love with something for that long.
The broken-fenced back alleys of tenements'
only beauty is the beauty of someone
who's said, *to hell with it, this is who I am.*
And that's not who I was in '78,
ten years after Tunis Ponsen died
largely ignored after early success,
in part because his subjects were too modest.
Now his paintings have come out of basements,
and a gallery show reminds me how
the slate-gray waves of Lake Michigan made
the best melancholy background for walking
to Union Station for those Sunday trips home.

In his last self-portrait, Ponsen painted
himself without any background at all.
He could be a brown-suited salesman, an
insurance exec, or actuarial.
His painting of a cigarette left burning
beside an airmail delivery letter
on a windowsill overlooking rain
makes even the least attentive Sunday
art lover here for hors d'oeuvres stop and look.
Is love contained in that letter, or loss?
Ponsen crafted his palette carefully to
capture the balance of these two people
below his window walking away from
each other in that gray rain. Maybe fame
ain't so great; you don't know how many years
of it you'll have—whereas love and loss are
for forever, or at least your part of it.

The Dancing Girls of Blind River

We left Presque Isle, my brother and I,
took a bad bearing and sailed through False Detour
Passage on the wrong side of Cockburn Island
if we were to make Meldrum Bay by night.
As the wind died down, we drank and listened
for weather reports from Ontario.
　　　　This is how we found out there were dancing girls
in Blind River just across the North Channel.
God knows why we didn't change course,
why we weren't sirened by those angels in pasties
bumping and grinding for truck drivers on
their last leg of 17 to Sudbury.
　　　　We put in after dark, a storm boiling
up in the still air, our engine running
on Coleman fuel. We stayed there for two days,
saw a stupid rich kid from Cleveland almost
lose his father's yacht in the swells of that storm
instead of staying tied up on the islands.
　　　　It's tempting to think that everything becomes
clear in time. Looking back at the tangled skein
of test line and fishhooks, you think you see
how you should have followed the one who loved you
instead of chasing the one you loved, how
you should have let the world have its way with you.
　　　　We put in at four more ports before home
and snapped our mast while crossing Lake Huron.
If we were rich, we could have taken more time,
sailed only when the wind was right, and stuffed
money in the G-strings of dancing girls,
begging them to reveal it all to us.

The Fishermen

Out on the breakwater, they stake their places
firmly as gargoyles, supplicants, or women
watching over the tomb. Someone's chrome fish glued
to a tackle box symbolizes Christ, who
is not himself a fish, but life itself,
which is nothing without Christ, or fishing—
at least according to this school of belief.
At the foot of the pier, the city's raised a plaque
with the photos of those who have been swept
away without warning into the arms
(or fins, after all) of the Lord unaware.
Their lines angle out obliquely from poles
into the choppy water. This mystery
commands their attention more completely
than TV, backs turned to the lovers
strolling hand-in-hand to the lighthouse.
There's a limit to what they can catch, but I
don't know what it is or what they're fishing for.
I head towards shore behind an old man
wheeling a stack of plastic buckets lashed
to a battered golf bag pull-cart with all
the love of someone for his oxygen tank.
Who doesn't want to be able to breathe
the blue, unbearable air of heaven?
To which the fishermen would answer, "Ah, Jesus!"
and cast their weighted bait back under the waves.

Gnosticism as a Modern Construct

Late one afternoon, we watched the dragonflies
near the dock that now sank below,
instead of standing over, the lily pads.

They enraptured us with the way
they needled the air, until a swallow
caught the one we were watching and was gone.

One possibility is that we
simply go on praying; another
that Christ walked *into* the sea.

At other times, we watched the swallows,
graceful as they dove after insects invisible
save for the ripples they made.

Heraclitus, Chagall, *et al.*

The river is a river.
The house above it is a house,
a habitation, a dream embodied in bricks and shingles and drywall.
The park is a park and a green space,
except for the asphalt parking lot,
except for the plastic swing set.
The couple on the park bench are lovers
and heartbreak in waiting.
The sky is the sky, blue
for some scientifically explicable reason
I might know if my fourth grade Earth Science class had
consisted of something other than a field trip to the county dump
and a green cardboard box complete
with everything needed for experiments
save curiosity.
The cars are, of course, cars
and reminders of underachievement, expressions of hope
and heartbreak in waiting.
And this day is this day, a river,
a habitation, a dream built of sunlight and heartbreak, curiously
irreproducible despite having all the ingredients
save for a door that lets you back
in once you swim
through it (and just try
to disprove this) inexplicably
into blue air.

The Musical Fountain

Each night during tourist season,
it starts up just after dark
at the base of the sand dune they use to set
off the Coast Guard festival fireworks.
One night it's mostly show tunes, the next
an R&B, classical and pop blend—
recordings blared through loudspeakers always
heralded by the fanfare from
Thus Spake Zarathustra.
Across the harbor, the great sprays of water
lit up by colored floodlights dance
a computerized set of moves.
They look like spray from the hoses
of firemen rehearsing
a rescue choreographed by Balanchine.
From my study window, I can see just the pinnacle
of each jet when the music is at forte.
If they were gas jets, I would
be seeing just that burning tip
where the gas has gone from music to sunlight.
When the wind blows off-land
out toward the lake, I might
not hear it at all, I might
be half-asleep before I remember just what
left a hole of silence in the evening.
This year, I'm staying on past Labor Day.
Who wouldn't want to be from a place
where the fountain spouts hymns
on Sunday evenings?
Tonight "How Great Thou Art"—
wet flames dancing in the rain
punctuated by thunder.
I like both the lightning out
over Lake Michigan
and the fountain's tacky majesty.
They seem like competing theologies:

grace that you're given,
and grace you have to earn.
From here, both seem equally
within reach,
so I watch the storm even after the fountain winds down,
and set the alarm for work.

A Postelection Walk along the Lake
Grand Haven, Mich., 11/3/04

Today, the water's disconcertingly calm.
Not a single sail pierces the horizon,
nor is the port's channel birthing freighters.
The vaguely Phoenician footprints of seagulls
add to the epic, imponderable
poem about water, sand, and bird.
A few abandoned beach chairs, half-hidden
by dune-grass, wait for a final visit
from their vacation home owners, busy now
with earning my envy. The cloudless sky is,
nonetheless, gauzy, as always, with longing.
How many times have I come here for comfort?
Almost as many as the mussel shells
cluttering up the high-water mark.
So this, too, will be memory—disaster
recollected in tranquility.
I could crawl all the way to Chicago,
but turn back when I reach my favorite
house I'll never own. The pier reaches out
just far enough to let you fish or drown.
And on the high dune darkening the harbor,
angels lie down in the grass, just waiting
to herald the savior with their plywood wings.

Basho in Autumn

The old pond
A frog jumps in
The sound of water
                    —Basho, trans., R.H. Blyth

Rain is making yellow aspen leaves stand
out brightly on their slick branching limbs
and more so in the fallen constellations
they form on this newly paved stretch of wet road.
I'm trying to get used to my new bifocals,
which blend my nearsightedness and my far
and make everything seem dreamlike and unreal.
So that's why I'm driving the back roads home
while listening to a radio report
about prayer and the believers' belief
that there is heaven and hell and nothing
in between. Between me and Lake Michigan
are migrant-harvested farms, shuttered fruit
stands, the lovely dappled shoulders of dunes,
another long winter and uncertain spring.
During summer, I'll crowd the beach to swim
no matter how little the lake warms up.
Sometimes, though, I only float on the sun-warmed
surface and try not to disturb the cold
layers below with my graceless backstroke.
Sometimes, I stand knee-deep on a sandbar,
gathering myself up for the plunge.
Mostly, I no longer believe there's a god.
Maybe this is just my being unable
to see the invisible, something
there is no correcting, just as blessing
my throat with candles could not make me sing
like a golden-throated angel in the choir
of the seraphim, or even on-key.
Yet I enjoyed my croaking even if
not one of the other parishioners did.
And when the frog jumps into the old pond,

we know that only through the sound it makes.
The frog, unseen, startles the poet Basho
into the heavenly realm of awareness.
Or something like that. I can't say that I am
ever going to jump in again clothed
only in my own precious skin, but I did
once, though, so I might be wrong—or right.
I might be about to swing this chariot
down to park at the beach just to listen
to the waves and watch the bulldozers hard
at work clearing sand from the shoreline road
that separates the lake from steep facing dunes
and the summer homes closed up tight until spring.

Actuarial

The results of my recent
        blood test confirm it—
            nothing about me is abnormal:
I don't have hepatitis
        in any of its forms,
            gonorrhea or syphilis,
and the level of my alanine
        aminotransferase
            doesn't suggest
my liver is stressed.
        Even my thyroid,
            sluggish for years,
now gives a normal reading.
        My height is just one-half
            inch short of what
I've heard is average—
        my weight
            is right on chart.
Not even the data from
        the digital sphygmo-
            manometer I wore
for twenty-four hours
        straight showed any
            cause for concern,
and this year my income
        will equal almost
            exactly the state mean.
Once I saw a psychiatrist
        after a failed affair,
            but within a month we were
already up to adulthood, so
        he couldn't see where
            there was left to go.
I never walked Blake's excessive
        path to the Palace of Wisdom—
            witness my complete

lack of circus skills:
      no physical deformities for
         the sideshow,
no strong-man strength,
      no hermaphrodism,
         no sword-swallowing throat.
Nor can I juggle,
      tumble, or twist
         myself in unnatural ways.
I, therefore, cannot
      con the carney
         able to guess my weight in days.

The Evolution of the Martini

Each year you use a little bit
more gin and less vermouth.
The ratio is exactly this:
your age over your youth.

Paracme

The trees are changing color in August—
too soon, at least for this latitude.
Something must be wrong with them. I mean, okay,
discount how the cemetery oaks feel,
but what about the lindens in the park?
Disease has killed off most of the elms,
emerald borers besiege the ashes,
but this is something else altogether.
The tree guys are trying to save our maple,
but I have my doubts about the outcome. Maybe
less worry would help. Maybe standing still
with a head full of bare branches and empty
nests would be my ticket to satori.
Maybe I should again ingest some medicine
to see those rainbows latent in limbs waving
ecstatically as Shiva in the wind.
Or I could just go to the nursery
and buy a late-season sapling on sale.
I could call the utilities to find
out where the various dangers are buried.
I could cradle the burlap-wrapped roots
in my arms and lower them in the ground.
If only my heart were in it instead
of in my throat or up to its arteries
with weeds and vines and invasives, I would.
I mean, my back is still up to the task.

Alter Ego

Mother and I are sitting in Sam's Joint,
a restaurant just around the corner
from the small-town condo she used to live in,
before she had to move to the old folks home.
She doesn't remember her place anymore,
nor can she decide what she wants to eat,
so I order her the fish special and
a glass of her favorite white zinfandel.
Once upon a time this was the local
tavern whose real name I can't recall;
everybody knew it as Hank and Cooney's
after the two guys who owned and tended it.
Now the walls are covered with such kitsch
as faded photos, old board games, broken
tricycles, you name it, all sorts of stuff
that has also come unglued from memory.
We're sitting almost exactly where there used
to be a phone booth that had a dimpled tin
interior that looked as if someone with
a miniature ball-peen hammer had
tried desperately to hammer his way out,
ignoring the booth's neatly folding glass door.
I ignore it, too, and the intervening
years, so I can use it as a fitting
room to don an unlikely superhero
uniform to save my mother from
the effects of the kryptonite of time,
forgetting I am not immune myself.
Let me report, therefore, in my mild-
mannered way, that I brandished a napkin
like a paper cape to wipe my mother's chin,
having no other powers at my command.

Stereopticon Views of the Future

have the gauzy, nineteenth-century feeling
of hand-tinted photographs. The scenes

are static, yet compelling, ponderable
as a diorama of dreams. An ash

handle worn smooth from anonymous hands
folds down neatly on its polished brass hinge,

and the twin-image cards fit in their slot
with the solid *clack* of pasteboard against wood.

Seen in 3-D through thick square lenses,
even fluorescent, hard-edged offices seem

romantic as vanished gardens in Ceylon,
or nearly. Cars as yet unbought already

look quaint in the ways designers gave shape
to amorphous desire. And have you ever

seen so many familiar strangers, their lips
red as next season's late-blooming roses?

Held up like a Venetian festival's
feathered mask, these glimpses into a time

when the party-goer no longer is,
is not so easy to put down coyly.

Looking away, how stunning the present!—
breathtaking, and taking your breath away.

On the Passing of the Great Picture Palaces

Mother shopped for curtains at Herpelsheimers
while I watched Bond, *James* Bond, in *Thunderball*
at the shabby Majestic Theater.

The carpet was threadbare, the lobby's ancient
potted palms dusty and dying from neglect—
its crushed red velvet seats worn down to nubs.

Even in decline, they were monumental
as mansions left standing among slums,
or castles whose royal families' lives

are open every afternoon in summer.
Now nothing is heralded from their marquees;
their ticket booths are boarded up even though

once no funeral parlor was as plush.
I suppose that I am growing older.
I want an outdated modesty, which keeps

one foot on the bedroom floor during love scenes,
want the mighty Wurlitzer to play something
lovely before it's lowered from sight.

The *Sun*, The *Star*, *et al.*

It's not an easy job, keeping love safe
and out of the paparazzi's blinding eyes,
away from the waiters who are just waiting
for the bottles of ambrosia to go flat.
There are thieves like me who will want to steal
any happiness left unattended—though
I don't believe that will happen any more
than I believe the photos of aliens
shaking hands with the president, or children
born wearing their dead fathers' tattoos.
Still, I envy them, the late-night shoppers
standing enraptured at check-out counters
heeding Baudelaire's call to be always drunk.
They stare at those blurry, lurid photos
as though they were windows onto a world
where fame and amazement and love are wed,
and garters and flowers fall to all the guests.

The Apollo Missions

The *Grand Rapids Press* used to censor ads
for B-grade films by scratching a bra strap
across a woman's otherwise naked back.
This was to keep us from thinking about breasts,
from lustful, imaginary caresses,
from all the sins an idle mind is heir.
Usually the woman's hair was pulled
back by her ringless hands, the effect dulled
by that strap. Still, thirteen years old, I sat
pondering it all: the moon's dark side,
the huge cost it was taking to get there,
how somewhere seas were being pulled to tide,
though so far inland it was hard to believe that.

Some Notes Concerning Love
and *Hemmings Motor News*
for Sue

Sometimes, half-hidden behind snow fences along
potholed county roads past ancient baseball diamonds
whose facets have all gone weed-choked and the players
grown rheumy, or else distant with senility,
you'll see the salvage yards of old Fords and Chevys,
a few of whose parts might really have been of use
about a marriage-and-a-half of the owner's
life ago—or half a liver, two bookkeepers,
three bitter kids, however you want to measure.
Which is only to say that's how I long felt—
built for speed, loosed upon the world with hoopla,
and then no longer even in the breakdown lane.
I could feel something gnawing and making a nest
in the coils beneath the blue vinyl of my life.
That was the year I quit writing, when words seemed like
sad things constructed from a California case
that consisted entirely of consonants.
The world was thick and guttural, viscous as oil.
How then did I find myself walking hand-in-hand
with you along Main Street on the Fourth of July,
admiring a line of classic cars, desire
bright as a turquoise Thunderbird that not even
God could restore with more attention to detail?
Yet, who wants to be bound so tightly to the past?
Not me, unh uh, nope, not any more. I'm tired
of crawling along on my tread-worn hands and knees.
No, to hell with authentic chrome grilles and shift knobs.
All I want is tape and glue, a few bungee cords,
handwritten directions, some kisses, love, and you.

Errata

On page one, for "below," please read "above."
The whole first section should be section two.
On page three, for "ramshackle," please read "love."

The cigarette the ingénue smokes is not menthol, but clove.
The current section one should be in the second person: "you."
(For additional correction, please see above.)

For "wide choppy bay," imagine just a cove.
In the description of the sailboat, for "old," read "new,"
and the water-stained manifest should be a pledge of love.

Throughout section three, for "crow," read "dove."
Those men shoveling coal in the cellar's deep blue
gloom should be folding sails in the showroom above.

"Kiln" on page 50 should be "stove";
on the second page 50, for "vase," read "stew,"
and on 53, for "glaze," please read "love."

On the last page, for "decline," be sure to read "approve."
Farther down, since it's summer, for "hoar frost" read "dew."
Lastly, for "shadows cast below," read "light from above,"
and the author intended the remainder to be love.

The Richard Snyder Publication Series

This book is the twelfth in a series honoring the memory of Richard Snyder (1925-1986), poet, fiction writer, playwright and longtime professor of English at Ashland University. Snyder served for fifteen years as English Department chair and was co-founder (in 1969) and co-editor of the Ashland Poetry Press. He was also co-founder of the Creative Writing major at the school, one of the first on the undergraduate level in the country. In selecting the manuscript for this book, the editors kept in mind Snyder's tenacious dedication to craftsmanship and thematic integrity.

Editor Deborah Fleming screened for the 2008 contest, and Elton Glaser judged.

Snyder Award Winners:
1997: Wendy Battin for *Little Apocalypse*
1998: David Ray for *Demons in the Diner*
1999: Philip Brady for *Weal*
2000: Jan Lee Ande for *Instructions for Walking on Water*
2001: Corrinne Clegg Hales for *Separate Escapes*
2002: Carol Barrett for *Calling in the Bones*
2003: Vern Rutsala for *The Moment's Equation*
2004: Christine Gelineau for *Remorseless Loyalty*
2005: Benjamin S. Grossberg for *Underwater Lengths in a Single Breath*
2006: Lorna Knowles Blake for *Permanent Address*
2007: Helen Pruitt Wallace for *Shimming the Glass House*
2008: Marc J. Sheehan for *Vengeful Hymns*